Purple

Harvest

 🩶 *Guided Journal & Workbook*

A 30-Day Journey to Cultivate Self-Awareness, Growth, and Lasting Change

---

by Dr. Rashonda Harris
Founder, Purple Sheep Consulting

Aim to Inspire, NOT compete!

💜 A <u>Welcome</u> Reflection by Dr. Rashonda Harris

"Every seed of change begins with a choice. By opening this journal, you've already said yes to your growth, your healing, and your truth. This journey isn't about perfectionists planting with intention, watering with grace, and trusting that your harvest will come. Let's grow."

— Dr. Rashonda Harris

Inside these pages, you'll:

⟡ Explore your Purple Harvest Personality

🌱 Cultivate emotional intelligence and personal insight

🏆 Develop habits that empower your next level

🍃 Reflect, reset, and reimagine your purpose

This is your space.

Your truth, your pace, your evolution.

Welcome to your *Harvest*.

🌿 Introduction: How to Use This Journal

Before you begin this journey, it's important to **connect the roots of your growth with the concepts planted throughout the Purple Harvest movement**. This journal is a companion to the book, *Purple Harvest: Planting Goals, Growing Truths*, and is designed to help you apply its lessons through daily reflection and action.

To fully align with the intention behind this workbook, it is *strongly recommended* that you: ☑ Read the book *Purple Harvest: Planting Goals, Growing Truths*

☑ Take the **Purple Harvest Personality Test** to discover your dominant growth style

Whether you identify as a **Power Planter, Precision Planner, Dream Weaver, or Root Builder**, this journal will help you:

☑ Understand your personal growth style and how it shapes your success

☑ Strengthen emotional intelligence (EQ) to enhance decision-making and resilience

☑ Develop intentional habits that align with your Purple Harvest Personality

☑ Track your growth over 30 days to build consistency and momentum

📌 **How It Works:**

• Each day, you'll complete one **guided reflection or action step**

• Every week ends with a **progress review** to help you refine your focus

• The final section includes a **6-month growth plan** based on your personality insights.

☑ Take the Purple Harvest Personality Test to discover your dominant growth style.

👉 You can access the quiz through the official portal:
Go to www.PurpleSheepConsulting.com/mentoring. **You will need to create an account to access the test. (Scroll Down to "Harvest Personalities") or "Scan the QR code below."**

This is more than a journal—it's your daily soil for clarity, courage, and commitment.

🌱 Are you ready to harvest success?

Let's begin! 💜

💜 **Week 1: Self-Discovery & Your Purple Harvest Personality**

Day 1: Your Growth Mindset Check-In

📖 **Reflection Prompt:**

- What is one area of your life you want to **improve or grow** in right now?

- What has stopped you from making progress in this area before?

📝 **Action Step:** Write down **one goal** you will focus on in this journal.

Day 2: Discover Your Purple Harvest Personality

◆ Take the **Purple Harvest Personality Quiz** (included in the appendix). 🔍 Haven't taken the quiz yet?
You can access your free personality quiz as a reader of *Purple Harvest*.
☞ Go to www.PurpleSheepConsulting.com/mentoring **(Scroll Down to "Harvest Personalities")**
🔓 Use password: **111**

✦ *Angel Number 111: A sign of alignment, clarity, and the power of new beginnings*

◆ Read about your personality type and answer:

- What aspects of this personality resonate with me?

- What strengths do I recognize in myself?

- What challenges do I need to overcome?

📌 **Action Step:** Write down **3 strengths** and **2 areas for improvement**.

Day 3: Understanding Your Growth Triggers

📖 **Reflection Prompt:**

- What situations make me feel **motivated and energized**?

- What situations make me feel **stuck, anxious, or hesitant**?

📝 **Action Step:**

Identify one **trigger that holds you back** and write a strategy to manage it.

Day 4: Embracing Emotional Intelligence (EQ) for Growth

Emotional Intelligence Self-Assessment:

Rate yourself (1-5) on:

- ☑ Self-awareness: I understand my emotions and reactions.
- ☑ Self-regulation: I manage my emotions without letting them control me.
- ☑ Motivation: I stay committed even when I don't feel inspired.
- ☑ Empathy: I understand how others feel and respond with care.
- ☑ Social skills: I communicate well and build strong relationships.

Action Step:

Choose **one EQ area** to focus on this week and create a growth plan.

Day 5: Goal-Setting with Your Personality Type

- Read your personality section:

  - Power Planters: How can I slow down and plan more strategically?

  - Precision Planners: What's one risk I can take this month?

  - Dream Weavers: How can I improve consistency and follow-through?

  - Root Builders: What small step can I take today to build momentum?

Action Step:

Write a **goal tailored to your personality** using the **SMART** format (Specific, Measurable, Achievable, Relevant, Time-bound).

Day 6: Reframing Challenges into Growth Opportunities

📖 **Reflection Prompt:**

- What's one past failure that taught me an important lesson?

- How can I use that lesson to fuel my success now?

📝 **Action Step:**

Write a **Growth Reframe Statement:**

"Instead of seeing [challenge] as a setback, I will see it as an opportunity to [lesson learned]."

Day 7: Week 1 Review & Progress Tracker

☑ What did I learn about myself this week?

☑ What small action helped me feel successful?

☑ What is one thing I will adjust next week?

📌 **Action Step:**

Rate your **progress this week** (1-5) and write down **one key insight.**

Action Step:

💜 Week 2-4: Deep Dive into Your Purple Harvest Personality

Each week, you'll focus on **building habits, overcoming challenges, and strengthening emotional intelligence** based on your personality type.

Have you identified with your Purple Harvest Personality?
What aspects resonated with you the most, and why do you think those traits connected with where you are in your growth journey right now?

Are there moments when you find yourself leaning into another Purple Harvest Personality?

Reflect on how this flexibility has helped (or could help) you adapt, grow, or overcome challenges. Which personality traits do you want to activate more intentionally?

💜 Day 8: Inner Voice Check-In

What is your inner voice telling you today? Is it encouraging or critical? How can you reframe it to support your growth?

💜 Day 9: Confidence Builder

Write about a time you felt truly confident. What contributed to that feeling and how can you replicate it today?

💜 Day 10: Accountability Reflection

Who in your life holds you accountable? How do you respond to accountability?

💜 Day 11: Emotional Intelligence Inventory

How do you manage your emotions when under pressure? What emotion do you find most challenging to navigate?

💜 Day 12: Courage Over Comfort

Describe a recent situation where you chose comfort over courage. How would you handle it differently now?

🩶 Day 13: Action Check-In

What action have you been avoiding? Break it into smaller steps and commit to the first one.

💜 Day 14: Strengths Spotlight

What is one strength you often overlook? How can you use it more intentionally this week?

🩶 Day 15: Visualize Your Harvest

Close your eyes and visualize your success. What does your 'harvest' look like in 6 months?

.

🩶 Day 16: Personality in Action

How has your Purple Harvest Personality shown up in your actions this week?

💜 Day 17: Grit and Grace

Reflect on a challenge that required both perseverance and self-compassion. What did you learn?

🩶 Day 18: Resource Check

What internal and external resources are helping you grow right now?

💜 Day 19: Limiting Beliefs

What's one belief holding you back from reaching your next level? How can you rewrite that belief?

🩶 Day 20: Dream Expansion

If you had zero limitations, what would you dream for your life?

🩶 Day 21: Reset Rituals

What daily or weekly habits help you reset and realign? Are there new ones you'd like to try?

💜 Day 22: Meaningful Connections

Who in your circle truly inspires and energizes you? How can you nurture that connection?

 **Day 23: Gratitude Deep Dive**

List three things you're deeply grateful for and explain why.

🌱 Your Purple Harvest Personality: A Guide to Growth 💜

By now, you've discovered your **Purple Harvest Personality** — the growth style that most resonates with your approach to progress, planning, and purpose. But here's a truth we honor in this journey:

You are not limited to just one personality.

Each of us carries **elements of all four personalities**, and at different times in our lives, we lean into the one that serves us best in the moment. Think of your dominant personality as your **root**, and the others as branches that help you adapt, evolve, and thrive.

Use this guide to recognize your dominant traits and know when to flex into another type for balance, momentum, or pause.

🌱 Purple Power Planter – *The Bold Doer*

You move with confidence and conviction. Once you plant a seed, you're already envisioning the bloom. You thrive on action, momentum, and quick decisions. Your challenge? Slow down enough to nurture your plans with structure.

📋 Purple Precision Planner – *The Strategic Organizer*

Your superpower is foresight. You prefer clarity before movement and map out the road before taking the first step. You are dependable, wise, and intentional. Your challenge? Trust your instincts even when the plan isn't perfect.

✨ Purple Dream Weaver – *The Visionary Creator*

You see the future in vivid color. Imagination and passion fuel your ideas, and you inspire others with your big-picture thinking. Your challenge? Turn dreams into consistent, grounded actions.

🌍 Purple Root Builder – *The Thoughtful Foundation Layer*

You grow slow but strong. You are deeply intentional, patient, and rooted in values that matter. Once committed, you endure. Your challenge? Don't wait for perfect conditions—start now and build as you go.

Reminder: Your personality is a **tool, not a label**. Let it **guide** you, not **define** you. Embrace your dominant personality but also trust yourself to reach for the one that aligns with the moment you're growing through. 🌿 🖤

BONUS ● **Power Planter Focus:**

Strength: Quick action, resilience, adaptability.

⚠ Challenge: Needs to slow down and create structured plans.

Weekly Goal: Develop **patience and strategic thinking.**

📖 Journal Prompts:

- What's one situation where I acted too quickly?

- How can I add **more structure** to my planning process?

- Who in my life models **strategic thinking**, and what can I learn from them?

📝 **Action Challenge:**

- Set a **72-hour waiting period** before making big decisions.

- Create a **detailed plan** before acting on a new goal.

BONUS ● **Precision Planner Focus:**

Strength: Analytical, organized, detail-oriented.

Challenge: Needs to take more risks and trust intuition.

Weekly Goal: Overcome **perfectionism and analysis paralysis.**

Journal Prompts:

- What's a decision I've delayed due to overthinking?

- What's the worst that could happen if I take action today?

- How can I **trust my instincts more**?

Action Challenge:

- Make a **small decision in 5 minutes** without overanalyzing.

- Take **one action step** on a project you've been planning for too long.

BONUS ● **Dream Weaver Focus:**

Strength: Creative, visionary, passionate.

Challenge: Needs consistency and follow-through.

Weekly Goal: Build **structure and accountability**.

Journal Prompts:

- What's one goal I started but didn't finish? Why?

- How can I break my **big ideas** into smaller, actionable steps?

- What **accountability system** can help me stay consistent?

Action Challenge:

- Set a **daily or weekly progress tracker** for your goal.

- Find an **accountability partner** to check in with.

BONUS ● **Purple Root Builder Focus:**

🪨 Strength: Thoughtful, deliberate, values quality.

⚠ Challenge: Needs to take **quicker action and build momentum.**

🔸 Weekly Goal: Start before feeling "ready."

📖 Journal Prompts:

- What's one goal I've put off for too long?

- How can I create **urgency** and take action this week?

- What is my **biggest fear about starting**, and how can I work through it?

📝 **Action Challenge:**

- Do **one uncomfortable action** related to your goal today.

- Set a **self-imposed deadline** for a project you've delayed.

💜 Day 24: Embracing Change

How do you typically respond to change? Reflect on a time when change led to unexpected growth.

💜 Day 25: Inner Critic vs Inner Coach

Write a dialogue between your inner critic and your inner coach. Who wins and why?

💜 Day 26: Lead with Purpose

How are you showing up as a leader in your own life?

🩶 Day 27: Celebrate Your Growth

What growth or wins have you noticed since starting this journal?
Celebrate them in detail.

💜 Day 28: Next Level You

Describe the version of yourself you're becoming. What are their habits, mindset, and lifestyle?

💜 Day 29: The Power of Pause

When was the last time you slowed down and truly rested? What does rest mean to you?

💜 Day 30: Harvest Reflection

Look back on this 30-day journey. What seeds did you plant, what grew, and what are you ready to harvest?

Congratulations

on Completing Your 30-Day Journey! 🎊 🌿 🖤

You showed up—for your growth, your healing, and your truth.

Over the past 30 days, you planted seeds of self-reflection, nurtured new habits, and began to harvest the first fruits of your transformation. You've not only discovered your Purple Harvest Personality—you've embodied it and learned how to tap into every version of you that serves your journey forward.

This wasn't just a journal.
It was a mirror.
A guide.
A soft landing.
And a bold launchpad.

"Transformation begins with intention—but it's sustained by consistent, loving action. And that's exactly what you've done."

— Dr. Rashonda Harris

Celebrate this moment.

Carry your harvest with pride.

And remember—this is only the beginning.

Driven by Excellence!

🩶 *The Purple Sheep Consulting Team*

🌱 Final Reflection: The Harvest & Long-Term Growth Plan

📖 Final Reflection Questions:

- ✅ What habits or mindset shifts have helped me the most?
- ✅ What strengths have I embraced in my Purple Harvest Personality?
- ✅ How will I **continue my growth** beyond this journal?

📝 Action Step:

- Write a **6-month action plan** for personal and professional growth.

- Set a **date to revisit this journal** in 3 months for a check-in.

🎉 Conclusion: Keep Planting & Growing!

Your journey doesn't stop here! Growth is a **lifelong harvest**—keep planting, nurturing, and evolving.

"In just 30 days, you didn't just complete a journal—you cultivated a new rhythm. You choose yourself, one page at a time. The seeds you planted are now habits taking root. Nurture them, trust their growth, and know this: a new beginning doesn't wait for permission—you just gave it to yourself."

— Dr. Rashonda Harris

Made in the USA
Middletown, DE
07 June 2025

76687599R00097